The Poetry of Henry Wadsworth Longfellow

Volume I – The Hanging of the Crane & Other Poems

Henry Wadsworth Longfellow was born on February 27th, 1807 in Portland, Maine. As a young boy, it was obvious that he was very studious and he quickly became fluent in Latin.

He published his first poem, "The Battle of Lovell's Pond", in the Portland Gazette on November 17th, 1820. He was already thinking of a career in literature and, in his senior year, wrote to his father: "I will not disguise it in the least... the fact is, I most eagerly aspire after future eminence in literature, my whole soul burns most ardently after it, and every earthly thought centers in it...."

After graduation travels in Europe occupied the next three years and he seemed to easily absorb any language he set himself to learn.

On September 14th, 1831, Longfellow married Mary Storer Potter. They settled in Brunswick.

His first published book was in 1833, a translation of poems by the Spanish poet Jorge Manrique. He also published a travel book, Outre-Mer: A Pilgrimage Beyond the Sea.

During a trip to Europe Mary became pregnant. Sadly, in October 1835, she miscarried at some six months. After weeks of illness she died, at the age of 22 on November 29th, 1835. Longfellow wrote "One thought occupies me night and day... She is dead — She is dead! All day I am weary and sad".

In late 1839, Longfellow published Hyperion, a book in prose inspired by his trips abroad.

Ballads and Other Poems was published in 1841 and included "The Village Blacksmith" and "The Wreck of the Hesperus". His reputation as a poet, and a commercial one at that, was set.

On May 10th, 1843, after seven years in pursuit of a chance for new love, Longfellow received word from Fanny Appleton that she agreed to marry him.

On November 1st, 1847, the epic poem Evangeline was published.

In 1854, Longfellow retired from Harvard, to devote himself entirely to writing.

The Song of Haiwatha, perhaps his best known and enjoyed work was published in 1855.

On July 10th, 1861, after suffering horrific burns the previous day. In his attempts to save her Longfellow had also been badly burned and was unable to attend her funeral.

He spent several years translating Dante Alighieri's Divine Comedy. It was published in 1867.

Longfellow was also part of a group who became known as The Fireside Poets which also included William Cullen Bryant, John Greenleaf Whittier, James Russell Lowell, and Oliver Wendell Holmes Snr.

Longfellow was the most popular poet of his day. As a friend once wrote to him, "no other poet was so fully recognized in his lifetime". Some of his works including "Paul Revere's Ride" and "The Song of Haiwatha" may have rewritten the facts but became essential parts of the American psyche and culture.

Henry Wadsworth Longfellow died, surrounded by family, on Friday, March 24th, 1882. He had been suffering from peritonitis.

Index of Contents

THE HANGING OF THE CRANE

I

The lights are out, and gone are all the guests
That thronging came with merriment and jests
To celebrate the Hanging of the Crane
In the new house,—into the night are gone;
But still the fire upon the hearth burns on,
And I alone remain.

O fortunate, O happy day,
When a new household finds its place
Among the myriad homes of earth,
Like a new star just sprung to birth,
And rolled on its harmonious way
Into the boundless realms of space!

So said the guests in speech and song,
As in the chimney, burning bright,

We hung the iron crane to-night,
And merry was the feast and long.

II

And now I sit and muse on what may be,
And in my vision see, or seem to see,
Through floating vapors interfused with light,
Shapes indeterminate, that gleam and fade,
As shadows passing into deeper shade
Sink and elude the sight.

For two alone, there in the hall,
As spread the table round and small;
Upon the polished silver shine
The evening lamps, but, more divine,
The light of love shines over all;
Of love, that says not mine and thine,
But ours, for ours is thine and mine.

They want no guests, to come between
Their tender glances like a screen,
And tell them tales of land and sea,
And whatsoever may betide
The great, forgotten world outside;
They want no guests; they needs must be
Each other's own best company.

III

The picture fades; as at a village fair
A showman's views, dissolving into air,
Again appear transfigured on the screen,
So in my fancy this; and now once more,
In part transfigured, through the open door
Appears the selfsame scene.

Seated, I see the two again,
But not alone; they entertain
A little angel unaware,
With face as round as is the moon;
A royal guest with flaxen hair,
Who, throned upon his lofty chair,
Drums on the table with his spoon,
Then drops it careless on the floor,
To grasp at things unseen before.

Are these celestial manners? these
The ways that win, the arts that please?
Ah yes; consider well the guest,
And whatsoe'er he does seems best;
He ruleth by the right divine
Of helplessness, so lately born
In purple chambers of the morn,
As sovereign over thee and thine.
He speaketh not; and yet there lies
A conversation in his eyes;
The golden silence of the Greek,
The gravest wisdom of the wise,
Not spoken in language, but in looks
More legible than printed books,
As if he could but would not speak.
And now, O monarch absolute,
Thy power is put to proof; for, lo!
Resistless, fathomless, and slow,
The nurse comes rustling like the sea,
And pushes back thy chair and thee,
And so good night to King Canute.

IV

As one who walking in a forest sees
A lovely landscape through the parted frees,
Then sees it not, for boughs that intervene
Or as we see the moon sometimes revealed
Through drifting clouds, and then again concealed,
So I behold the scene.

There are two guests at table now;
The king, deposed and older grown,
No longer occupies the throne,—
The crown is on his sister's brow;
A Princess from the Fairy Isles,
The very pattern girl of girls.
All covered and embowered in curls,
Rose-tinted from the Isle of Flowers,
And sailing with soft, silken sails
From far-off Dreamland into ours.
Above their bowls with rims of blue
Four azure eyes of deeper hue
Are looking, dreamy with delight;
Limpid as planets that emerge
Above the ocean's rounded verge,

Soft-shining through the summer night.
Steadfast they gaze, yet nothing see
Beyond the horizon of their bowls;
Nor care they for the world that rolls
With all its freight of troubled souls
Into the days that are to be.

V

Again the tossing boughs shut out the scene,
Again the drifting vapors intervene,
And the moon's pallid disk is hidden quite;
And now I see the table wider grown,
As round a pebble into water thrown
Dilates a ring of light.

I see the table wider grown,
I see it garlanded with guests,
As if fair Ariadne's Crown
Out of the sky had fallen down;
Maidens within whose tender breasts
A thousand restless hopes and fears,
Forth reaching to the coming years,
Flutter awhile, then quiet lie
Like timid birds that fain would fly,
But do not dare to leave their nests;—
And youths, who in their strength elate
Challenge the van and front of fate,
Eager as champions to be
In the divine knight-errantry
Of youth, that travels sea and land
Seeking adventures, or pursues,
Through cities, and through solitudes
Frequented by the lyric Muse,
The phantom with the beckoning hand,
That still allures and still eludes.
O sweet illusions of the brain!
O sudden thrills of fire and frost!
The world is bright while ye remain,
And dark and dead when ye are lost!

VI

The meadow-brook, that seemeth to stand still,
Quickens its current as it nears the mill;
And so the stream of Time that lingereth

In level places, and so dull appears,
Runs with a swifter current as it nears
The gloomy mills of Death.

And now, like the magician's scroll,
That in the owner's keeping shrinks
With every wish he speaks or thinks,
Till the last wish consumes the whole,
The table dwindles, and again
I see the two alone remain.
The crown of stars is broken in parts;
Its jewels, brighter than the day,
Have one by one been stolen away
To shine in other homes and hearts.
One is a wanderer now afar
In Ceylon or in Zanzibar,
Or sunny regions of Cathay;
And one is in the boisterous camp
Mid clink of arms and horses' tramp,
And battle's terrible array.
I see the patient mother read,
With aching heart, of wrecks that float
Disabled on those seas remote,
Or of some great heroic deed
On battle-fields where thousands bleed
To lift one hero into fame.
Anxious she bends her graceful head
Above these chronicles of pain,
And trembles with a secret dread
Lest there among the drowned or slain
She find the one beloved name.

VII

After a day of cloud and wind and rain
Sometimes the setting sun breaks out again,
And touching all the darksome woods with light,
Smiles on the fields, until they laugh and sing,
Then like a ruby from the horizon's ring
Drops down into the night.

What see I now? The night is fair,
The storm of grief, the clouds of care,
The wind, the rain, have passed away;
The lamps are lit, the fires burn bright,
The house is full of life and light:
It is the Golden Wedding day.

The guests come thronging in once more,
Quick footsteps sound along the floor,
The trooping children crowd the stair,
And in and out and everywhere
Flashes along the corridor
The sunshine of their golden hair.
On the round table in the hall
Another Ariadne's Crown
Out of the sky hath fallen down;
More than one Monarch of the Moon
Is drumming with his silver spoon;
The light of love shines over all.

O fortunate, O happy day!
The people sing, the people say.
The ancient bridegroom and the bride,
Smiling contented and serene
Upon the blithe, bewildering scene,
Behold, well pleased, on every side
Their forms and features multiplied,
As the reflection of a light
Between two burnished mirrors gleams,
Or lamps upon a bridge at night
Stretch on and on before the sight,
Till the long vista endless seems.

MORITURI SALUTAMUS

POEM FOR THE FIFTIETH ANNIVERSARY OF THE CLASS OF 1825 IN BOWDOIN COLLEGE

Tempora labuntur, tacitisque senescimus annis,
Et fugiunt freno non remorante dies. —**OVID**

"O Caesar, we who are about to die
Salute you!" was the gladiators' cry
In the arena, standing face to face
With death and with the Roman populace.

O ye familiar scenes,—ye groves of pine,
That once were mine and are no longer mine,—
Thou river, widening through the meadows green
To the vast sea, so near and yet unseen,—
Ye halls, in whose seclusion and repose
Phantoms of fame, like exhalations, rose
And vanished,—we who are about to die
Salute you; earth and air and sea and sky,

And the Imperial Sun that scatters down
His sovereign splendors upon grove and town.

Ye do not answer us! ye do not hear!
We are forgotten; and in your austere
And calm indifference, ye little care
Whether we come or go, or whence or where.
What passing generations fill these halls,
What passing voices echo front these walls,
Ye heed not; we are only as the blast,
A moment heard, and then forever past.

Not so the teachers who in earlier days
Led our bewildered feet through learning's maze;
They answer us—alas! what have I said?
What greetings come there from the voiceless dead?
What salutation, welcome, or reply?
What pressure from the hands that lifeless lie?
They are no longer here; they all are gone
Into the land of shadows,—all save one.
Honor and reverence, and the good repute
That follows faithful service as its fruit,
Be unto him, whom living we salute.

The great Italian poet, when he made
His dreadful journey to the realms of shade,
Met there the old instructor of his youth,
And cried in tones of pity and of ruth:
"O, never from the memory of my heart
Your dear, paternal image shall depart,
Who while on earth, ere yet by death surprised,
Taught me how mortals are immortalized;
How grateful am I for that patient care
All my life long my language shall declare."

To-day we make the poet's words our own
And utter them in plaintive undertone;
Nor to the living only be they said,
But to the other living called the dead,
Whose dear, paternal images appear
Not wrapped in gloom, but robed in sunshine here;
Whose simple lives, complete and without flaw,
Were part and parcel of great Nature's law;
Who said not to their Lord, as if afraid
"Here is thy talent in a napkin laid,"
But labored in their sphere, as men who live
In the delight that work alone can give.
Peace be to them; eternal peace and rest,

And the fulfilment of the great behest:
"Ye have been faithful over a few things,
Over ten cities shall ye reign as kings."

And ye who fill the places we once filled,
And follow in the furrows that we tilled,
Young men, whose generous hearts are beating high,
We who are old, and are about to die,
Salute you; hail you; take your hands in ours,
And crown you with our welcome as with flowers!
How beautiful is youth! how bright it gleams
With its illusions, aspirations, dreams!
Book of Beginnings, Story without End,
Each maid a heroine, and each man a friend!
Aladdin's Lamp, and Fortunatus' Purse,
That holds the treasures of the universe!
All possibilities are in its hands,
No danger daunts it, and no foe withstands;
In its sublime audacity of faith,
"Be thou removed!" it to the mountain saith,
And with ambitious feet, secure and proud,
Ascends the ladder leaning on the cloud!

As ancient Priam at the Scaean gate
Sat on the walls of Troy in regal state
With the old men, too old and weak to fight,
Chirping like grasshoppers in their delight
To see the embattled hosts, with spear and shield,
Of Trojans and Achaians in the field;
So from the snowy summits of our years
We see you in the plain, as each appears,
And question of you; asking, "Who is he
That towers above the others? Which may be
Atreides, Menelaus, Odysseus,
Ajax the great, or bold Idomeneus?"

Let him not boast who puts his armor on
As he who puts it off, the battle done.
Study yourselves; and most of all note well
Wherein kind Nature meant you to excel.
Not every blossom ripens into fruit;
Minerva, the inventress of the flute,
Flung it aside, when she her face surveyed
Distorted in a fountain as she played;
The unlucky Marsyas found it, and his fate
Was one to make the bravest hesitate.

Write on your doors the saying wise and old,

"Be bold! be bold!" and everywhere—"Be bold;
Be not too bold!" Yet better the excess
Than the defect; better the more than less;
Better like Hector in the field to die,
Than like a perfumed Paris turn and fly,

And now, my classmates; ye remaining few
That number not the half of those we knew,
Ye, against whose familiar names not yet
The fatal asterisk of death is set,
Ye I salute! The horologe of Time
Strikes the half-century with a solemn chime,
And summons us together once again,
The joy of meeting not unmixed with pain.

Where are the others? Voices from the deep
Caverns of darkness answer me: "They sleep!"
I name no names; instinctively I feel
Each at some well-remembered grave will kneel,
And from the inscription wipe the weeds and moss,
For every heart best knoweth its own loss.
I see their scattered gravestones gleaming white
Through the pale dusk of the impending night;
O'er all alike the impartial sunset throws
Its golden lilies mingled with the rose;
We give to each a tender thought, and pass
Out of the graveyards with their tangled grass,
Unto these scenes frequented by our feet
When we were young, and life was fresh and sweet.

What shall I say to you? What can I say
Better than silence is? When I survey
This throng of faces turned to meet my own,
Friendly and fair, and yet to me unknown,
Transformed the very landscape seems to be;
It is the same, yet not the same to me.
So many memories crowd upon my brain,
So many ghosts are in the wooded plain,
I fain would steal away, with noiseless tread,
As from a house where some one lieth dead.
I cannot go;—I pause;—I hesitate;
My feet reluctant linger at the gate;
As one who struggles in a troubled dream
To speak and cannot, to myself I seem.

Vanish the dream! Vanish the idle fears!
Vanish the rolling mists of fifty years!
Whatever time or space may intervene,

I will not be a stranger in this scene.
Here every doubt, all indecision, ends;
Hail, my companions, comrades, classmates, friends!

Ah me! the fifty years since last we met
Seem to me fifty folios bound and set
By Time, the great transcriber, on his shelves,
Wherein are written the histories of ourselves.
What tragedies, what comedies, are there;
What joy and grief, what rapture and despair!
What chronicles of triumph and defeat,
Of struggle, and temptation, and retreat!
What records of regrets, and doubts, and fears
What pages blotted, blistered by our tears!
What lovely landscapes on the margin shine,
What sweet, angelic faces, what divine
And holy images of love and trust,
Undimmed by age, unsoiled by damp or dust!

Whose hand shall dare to open and explore
These volumes, closed and clasped forevermore?
Not mine. With reverential feet I pass;
I hear a voice that cries, "Alas! alas!
Whatever hath been written shall remain,
Nor be erased nor written o'er again;
The unwritten only still belongs to thee:
Take heed, and ponder well what that shall be."

As children frightened by a thundercloud
Are reassured if some one reads aloud
A tale of wonder, with enchantment fraught,
Or wild adventure, that diverts their thought,
Let me endeavor with a tale to chase
The gathering shadows of the time and place,
And banish what we all too deeply feel
Wholly to say, or wholly to conceal.

In mediaeval Rome, I know not where,
There stood an image with its arm in air,
And on its lifted finger, shining clear,
A golden ring with the device, "Strike here!"
Greatly the people wondered, though none guessed
The meaning that these words but half expressed,
Until a learned clerk, who at noonday
With downcast eyes was passing on his way,
Paused, and observed the spot, and marked it well,
Whereon the shadow of the finger fell;
And, coming back at midnight, delved, and found

A secret stairway leading under ground.
Down this he passed into a spacious hall,
Lit by a flaming jewel on the wall;
And opposite in threatening attitude
With bow and shaft a brazen statue stood.
Upon its forehead, like a coronet,
Were these mysterious words of menace set:
"That which I am, I am; my fatal aim
None can escape, not even yon luminous flame!"

Midway the hall was a fair table placed,
With cloth of gold, and golden cups enchased
With rubies, and the plates and knives were gold,
And gold the bread and viands manifold.
Around it, silent, motionless, and sad,
Were seated gallant knights in armor clad,
And ladies beautiful with plume and zone,
But they were stone, their hearts within were stone;
And the vast hall was filled in every part
With silent crowds, stony in face and heart.

Long at the scene, bewildered and amazed
The trembling clerk in speechless wonder gazed;
Then from the table, by his greed made bold,
He seized a goblet and a knife of gold,
And suddenly from their seats the guests upsprang,
The vaulted ceiling with loud clamors rang,
The archer sped his arrow, at their call,
Shattering the lambent jewel on the wall,
And all was dark around and overhead;—
Stark on the door the luckless clerk lay dead!

The writer of this legend then records
Its ghostly application in these words:
The image is the Adversary old,
Whose beckoning finger points to realms of gold;
Our lusts and passions are the downward stair
That leads the soul from a diviner air;
The archer, Death; the flaming jewel, Life;
Terrestrial goods, the goblet and the knife;
The knights and ladies, all whose flesh and bone
By avarice have been hardened into stone;
The clerk, the scholar whom the love of pelf
Tempts from his books and from his nobler self.

The scholar and the world! The endless strife,
The discord in the harmonies of life!
The love of learning, the sequestered nooks,

And all the sweet serenity of books;
The market-place, the eager love of gain,
Whose aim is vanity, and whose end is pain!

But why, you ask me, should this tale be told
To men grown old, or who are growing old?
It is too late! Ah, nothing is too late
Till the tired heart shall cease to palpitate.
Cato learned Greek at eighty; Sophocles
Wrote his grand Oedipus, and Simonides
Bore off the prize of verse from his compeers,
When each had numbered more than fourscore years,
And Theophrastus, at fourscore and ten,
Had but begun his Characters of Men.
Chaucer, at Woodstock with the nightingales,
At sixty wrote the Canterbury Tales;
Goethe at Weimar, toiling to the last,
Completed Faust when eighty years were past.
These are indeed exceptions; but they show
How far the gulf-stream of our youth may flow
Into the arctic regions of our lives.
Where little else than life itself survives.

As the barometer foretells the storm
While still the skies are clear, the weather warm,
So something in us, as old age draws near,
Betrays the pressure of the atmosphere.
The nimble mercury, ere we are aware,
Descends the elastic ladder of the air;
The telltale blood in artery and vein
Sinks from its higher levels in the brain;
Whatever poet, orator, or sage
May say of it, old age is still old age.
It is the waning, not the crescent moon;
The dusk of evening, not the blaze of noon:
It is not strength, but weakness; not desire,
But its surcease; not the fierce heat of fire,
The burning and consuming element,
But that of ashes and of embers spent,
In which some living sparks we still discern,
Enough to warm, but not enough to burn.

What then? Shall we sit idly down and say
The night hath come; it is no longer day?
The night hath not yet come; we are not quite
Cut off from labor by the failing light;
Something remains for us to do or dare;
Even the oldest tree some fruit may bear;

Not Oedipus Coloneus, or Greek Ode,
Or tales of pilgrims that one morning rode
Out of the gateway of the Tabard inn,
But other something, would we but begin;
For age is opportunity no less
Than youth itself, though in another dress,
And as the evening twilight fades away
The sky is filled with stars, invisible by day.

A BOOK OF SONNETS

THREE FRIENDS OF MINE

I

When I remember them, those friends of mine,
Who are no longer here, the noble three,
Who half my life were more than friends to me,
And whose discourse was like a generous wine,
I most of all remember the divine
Something, that shone in them, and made us see
The archetypal man, and what might be
The amplitude of Nature's first design.
In vain I stretch my hands to clasp their hands;
I cannot find them. Nothing now is left
But a majestic memory. They meanwhile
Wander together in Elysian lands,
Perchance remembering me, who am bereft
Of their dear presence, and, remembering, smile.

II

In Attica thy birthplace should have been,
Or the Ionian Isles, or where the seas
Encircle in their arms the Cyclades,
So wholly Greek wast thou in thy serene
And childlike joy of life, O Philhellene!
Around thee would have swarmed the Attic bees;
Homer had been thy friend, or Socrates,
And Plato welcomed thee to his demesne.
For thee old legends breathed historic breath;
Thou sawest Poseidon in the purple sea,
And in the sunset Jason's fleece of gold!
O, what hadst thou to do with cruel Death,
Who wast so full of life, or Death with thee,

That thou shouldst die before thou hadst grown old!

III

I stand again on the familiar shore,
And hear the waves of the distracted sea
Piteously calling and lamenting thee,
And waiting restless at thy cottage door.
The rocks, the sea-weed on the ocean floor,
The willows in the meadow, and the free
Wild winds of the Atlantic welcome me;
Then why shouldst thou be dead, and come no more?
Ah, why shouldst thou be dead, when common men
Are busy with their trivial affairs,
Having and holding? Why, when thou hadst read
Nature's mysterious manuscript, and then
Wast ready to reveal the truth it bears,
Why art thou silent! Why shouldst thou be dead?

IV

River, that stealest with such silent pace
Around the City of the Dead, where lies
A friend who bore thy name, and whom these eyes
Shall see no more in his accustomed place,
Linger and fold him in thy soft embrace
And say good night, for now the western skies
Are red with sunset, and gray mists arise
Like damps that gather on a dead man's face.
Good night! good night! as we so oft have said
Beneath this roof at midnight in the days
That are no more, and shall no more return.
Thou hast but taken thy lamp and gone to bed;
I stay a little longer, as one stays
To cover up the embers that still burn.

V

The doors are all wide open; at the gate
The blossomed lilacs counterfeit a blaze,
And seem to warm the air; a dreamy haze
Hangs o'er the Brighton meadows like a fate,
And on their margin, with sea-tides elate,
The flooded Charles, as in the happier days,
Writes the last letter of his name, and stays

His restless steps, as if compelled to wait.
I also wait; but they will come no more,
Those friends of mine, whose presence satisfied
The thirst and hunger of my heart. Ah me!
They have forgotten the pathway to my door!
Something is gone from nature since they died,
And summer is not summer, nor can be.

CHAUCER

An old man in a lodge within a park;
The chamber walls depicted all around
With portraitures of huntsman, hawk, and hound.
And the hurt deer. He listeneth to the lark,
Whose song comes with the sunshine through the dark
Of painted glass in leaden lattice bound;
He listeneth and he laugheth at the sound,
Then writeth in a book like any clerk.
He is the poet of the dawn, who wrote
The Canterbury Tales, and his old age
Made beautiful with song; and as I read
I hear the crowing cock, I hear the note
Of lark and linnet, and from every page
Rise odors of ploughed field or flowery mead.

SHAKESPEARE

A vision as of crowded city streets,
With human life in endless overflow;
Thunder of thoroughfares; trumpets that blow
To battle; clamor, in obscure retreats,
Of sailors landed from their anchored fleets;
Tolling of bells in turrets, and below
Voices of children, and bright flowers that throw
O'er garden-walls their intermingled sweets!
This vision comes to me when I unfold
The volume of the Poet paramount,
Whom all the Muses loved, not one alone;—
Into his hands they put the lyre of gold,
And, crowned with sacred laurel at their fount,
Placed him as Musagetes on their throne.

MILTON

I pace the sounding sea-beach and behold
How the voluminous billows roll and run,
Upheaving and subsiding, while the sun
Shines through their sheeted emerald far unrolled,
And the ninth wave, slow gathering fold by fold
All its loose-flowing garments into one,
Plunges upon the shore, and floods the dun
Pale reach of sands, and changes them to gold.
So in majestic cadence rise and fall
The mighty undulations of thy song,
O sightless bard, England's Maeonides!
And ever and anon, high over all
Uplifted, a ninth wave superb and strong,
Floods all the soul with its melodious seas.

KEATS

The young Endymion sleeps Endymion's sleep;
The shepherd-boy whose tale was left half told!
The solemn grove uplifts its shield of gold
To the red rising moon, and loud and deep
The nightingale is singing from the steep;
It is midsummer, but the air is cold;
Can it be death? Alas, beside the fold
A shepherd's pipe lies shattered near his sheep.
Lo! in the moonlight gleams a marble white,
On which I read: "Here lieth one whose name
Was writ in water." And was this the meed
Of his sweet singing? Rather let me write:
"The smoking flax before it burst to flame
Was quenched by death, and broken the bruised reed."

THE GALAXY

Torrent of light and river of the air,
Along whose bed the glimmering stars are seen
Like gold and silver sands in some ravine
Where mountain streams have left their channels bare!
The Spaniard sees in thee the pathway, where
His patron saint descended in the sheen
Of his celestial armor, on serene
And quiet nights, when all the heavens were fair.

Not this I see, nor yet the ancient fable
Of Phaeton's wild course, that scorched the skies
Where'er the hoofs of his hot coursers trod;
But the white drift of worlds o'er chasms of sable,
The star-dust that is whirled aloft and flies
From the invisible chariot-wheels of God.

THE SOUND OF THE SEA

The sea awoke at midnight from its sleep,
And round the pebbly beaches far and wide
I heard the first wave of the rising tide
Rush onward with uninterrupted sweep;
A voice out of the silence of the deep,
A sound mysteriously multiplied
As of a cataract from the mountain's side,
Or roar of winds upon a wooded steep.
So comes to us at times, from the unknown
And inaccessible solitudes of being,
The rushing of the sea-tides of the soul;
And inspirations, that we deem our own,
Are some divine foreshadowing and foreseeing
Of things beyond our reason or control.

A SUMMER DAY BY THE SEA

The sun is set; and in his latest beams
Yon little cloud of ashen gray and gold,
Slowly upon the amber air unrolled,
The falling mantle of the Prophet seems.
From the dim headlands many a lighthouse gleams,
The street-lamps of the ocean; and behold,
O'erhead the banners of the night unfold;
The day hath passed into the land of dreams.
O summer day beside the joyous sea!
O summer day so wonderful and white,
So full of gladness and so full of pain!
Forever and forever shalt thou be
To some the gravestone of a dead delight,
To some the landmark of a new domain.

THE TIDES

I saw the long line of the vacant shore,
The sea-weed and the shells upon the sand,
And the brown rocks left bare on every hand,
As if the ebbing tide would flow no more.
Then heard I, more distinctly than before,
The ocean breathe and its great breast expand,
And hurrying came on the defenceless land
The insurgent waters with tumultuous roar.
All thought and feeling and desire, I said,
Love, laughter, and the exultant joy of song
Have ebbed from me forever! Suddenly o'er me
They swept again from their deep ocean bed,
And in a tumult of delight, and strong
As youth, and beautiful as youth, upbore me.

A SHADOW

I said unto myself, if I were dead,
What would befall these children? What would be
Their fate, who now are looking up to me
For help and furtherance? Their lives, I said,
Would be a volume wherein I have read
But the first chapters, and no longer see
To read the rest of their dear history,
So full of beauty and so full of dread.
Be comforted; the world is very old,
And generations pass, as they have passed,
A troop of shadows moving with the sun;
Thousands of times has the old tale been told;
The world belongs to those who come the last,
They will find hope and strength as we have done.

A NAMELESS GRAVE

"A soldier of the Union mustered out,"
Is the inscription on an unknown grave
At Newport News, beside the salt-sea wave,
Nameless and dateless; sentinel or scout
Shot down in skirmish, or disastrous rout
Of battle, when the loud artillery drave
Its iron wedges through the ranks of brave
And doomed battalions, storming the redoubt.
Thou unknown hero sleeping by the sea

In thy forgotten grave! with secret shame
I feel my pulses beat, my forehead burn,
When I remember thou hast given for me
All that thou hadst, thy life, thy very name,
And I can give thee nothing in return.

SLEEP

Lull me to sleep, ye winds, whose fitful sound
Seems from some faint Aeolian harp-string caught;
Seal up the hundred wakeful eyes of thought
As Hermes with his lyre in sleep profound
The hundred wakeful eyes of Argus bound;
For I am weary, and am overwrought
With too much toil, with too much care distraught,
And with the iron crown of anguish crowned.
Lay thy soft hand upon my brow and cheek,
O peaceful Sleep! until from pain released
I breathe again uninterrupted breath!
Ah, with what subtile meaning did the Greek
Call thee the lesser mystery at the feast
Whereof the greater mystery is death!

THE OLD BRIDGE AT FLORENCE

Taddeo Gaddi built me. I am old,
Five centuries old. I plant my foot of stone
Upon the Arno, as St. Michael's own
Was planted on the dragon. Fold by fold
Beneath me as it struggles. I behold
Its glistening scales. Twice hath it overthrown
My kindred and companions. Me alone
It moveth not, but is by me controlled,
I can remember when the Medici
Were driven from Florence; longer still ago
The final wars of Ghibelline and Guelf.
Florence adorns me with her jewelry;
And when I think that Michael Angelo
Hath leaned on me, I glory in myself.

IL PONTE VECCHIO DI FIRENZE

Gaddi mi fece; il Ponte Vecchio sono;
Cinquecent' anni gia sull' Arno pianto
Il piede, come il suo Michele Santo
Pianto sul draco. Mentre ch' io ragiono
Lo vedo torcere con flebil suono
Le rilucenti scaglie. Ha questi affranto
Due volte i miei maggior. Me solo intanto
Neppure muove, ed io non l' abbandono.
Io mi rammento quando fur cacciati
I Medici; pur quando Ghibellino
E Guelfo fecer pace mi rammento.
Fiorenza i suoi giojelli m' ha prestati;
E quando penso ch' Agnolo il divino
Su me posava, insuperbir mi sento.

NATURE

As a fond mother, when the day is o'er,
Leads by the hand her little child to bed,
Half willing, half reluctant to be led,
And leave his broken playthings on the floor,
Still gazing at them through the open door,
Nor wholly reassured and comforted
By promises of others in their stead,
Which, though more splendid, may not please him more;
So Nature deals with us, and takes away
Our playthings one by one, and by the hand
Leads us to rest so gently, that we go
Scarce knowing if we wish to go or stay,
Being too full of sleep to understand
How far the unknown transcends the what we know.

IN THE CHURCHYARD AT TARRYTOWN

Here lies the gentle humorist, who died
In the bright Indian Summer of his fame!
A simple stone, with but a date and name,
Marks his secluded resting-place beside
The river that he loved and glorified.
Here in the autumn of his days he came,
But the dry leaves of life were all aflame
With tints that brightened and were multiplied.
How sweet a life was his; how sweet a death!
Living, to wing with mirth the weary hours,

Or with romantic tales the heart to cheer;
Dying, to leave a memory like the breath
Of summers full of sunshine and of showers,
A grief and gladness in the atmosphere.

ELIOT'S OAK

Thou ancient oak! whose myriad leaves are loud
With sounds of unintelligible speech,
Sounds as of surges on a shingly beach,
Or multitudinous murmurs of a crowd;
With some mysterious gift of tongues endowed,
Thou speakest a different dialect to each;
To me a language that no man can teach,
Of a lost race, long vanished like a cloud.
For underneath thy shade, in days remote,
Seated like Abraham at eventide
Beneath the oaks of Mamre, the unknown
Apostle of the Indians, Eliot, wrote
His Bible in a language that hath died
And is forgotten, save by thee alone.

THE DESCENT OF THE MUSES

Nine sisters, beautiful in form and face,
Came from their convent on the shining heights
Of Pierus, the mountain of delights,
To dwell among the people at its base.
Then seemed the world to change. All time and space,
Splendor of cloudless days and starry nights,
And men and manners, and all sounds and sights,
Had a new meaning, a diviner grace.
Proud were these sisters, but were not too proud
To teach in schools of little country towns
Science and song, and all the arts that please;
So that while housewives span, and farmers ploughed,
Their comely daughters, clad in homespun gowns,
Learned the sweet songs of the Pierides.

VENICE

White swan of cities, slumbering in thy nest

So wonderfully built among the reeds
Of the lagoon, that fences thee and feeds,
As sayeth thy old historian and thy guest!
White water-lily, cradled and caressed
By ocean streams, and from the silt and weeds
Lifting thy golden filaments and seeds,
Thy sun-illumined spires, thy crown and crest!
White phantom city, whose untrodden streets
Are rivers, and whose pavements are the shifting
Shadows of palaces and strips of sky;
I wait to see thee vanish like the fleets
Seen in mirage, or towers of cloud uplifting
In air their unsubstantial masonry.

THE POETS

O ye dead Poets, who are living still
Immortal in your verse, though life be fled,
And ye, O living Poets, who are dead
Though ye are living, if neglect can kill,
Tell me if in the darkest hours of ill,
With drops of anguish falling fast and red
From the sharp crown of thorns upon your head,
Ye were not glad your errand to fulfil?
Yes; for the gift and ministry of Song
Have something in them so divinely sweet,
It can assuage the bitterness of wrong;
Not in the clamor of the crowded street,
Not in the shouts and plaudits of the throng,
But in ourselves, are triumph and defeat.

PARKER CLEAVELAND

WRITTEN ON REVISITING BRUNSWICK IN THE SUMMER OF 1875

Among the many lives that I have known,
None I remember more serene and sweet,
More rounded in itself and more complete,
Than his, who lies beneath this funeral stone.
These pines, that murmur in low monotone,
These walks frequented by scholastic feet,
Were all his world; but in this calm retreat
For him the Teacher's chair became a throne.
With fond affection memory loves to dwell

On the old days, when his example made
A pastime of the toil of tongue and pen;
And now, amid the groves he loved so well
That naught could lure him from their grateful shade,
He sleeps, but wakes elsewhere, for God hath said, Amen!

THE HARVEST MOON

It is the Harvest Moon! On gilded vanes
And roofs of villages, on woodland crests
And their aerial neighborhoods of nests
Deserted, on the curtained window-panes
Of rooms where children sleep, on country lanes
And harvest-fields, its mystic splendor rests!
Gone are the birds that were our summer guests,
With the last sheaves return the laboring wains!
All things are symbols: the external shows
Of Nature have their image in the mind,
As flowers and fruits and falling of the leaves;
The song-birds leave us at the summer's close,
Only the empty nests are left behind,
And pipings of the quail among the sheaves.

TO THE RIVER RHONE

Thou Royal River, born of sun and shower
In chambers purple with the Alpine glow,
Wrapped in the spotless ermine of the snow
And rocked by tempests!—at the appointed hour
Forth, like a steel-clad horseman from a tower,
With clang and clink of harness dost thou go
To meet thy vassal torrents, that below
Rush to receive thee and obey thy power.
And now thou movest in triumphal march,
A king among the rivers! On thy way
A hundred towns await and welcome thee;
Bridges uplift for thee the stately arch,
Vineyards encircle thee with garlands gay,
And fleets attend thy progress to the sea!

THE THREE SILENCES OF MOLINOS

TO JOHN GREENLEAF WHITTIER

Three Silences there are: the first of speech,
The second of desire, the third of thought;
This is the lore a Spanish monk, distraught
With dreams and visions, was the first to teach.
These Silences, commingling each with each,
Made up the perfect Silence, that he sought
And prayed for, and wherein at times he caught
Mysterious sounds from realms beyond our reach.
O thou, whose daily life anticipates
The life to come, and in whose thought and word
The spiritual world preponderates.
Hermit of Amesbury! thou too hast heard
Voices and melodies from beyond the gates,
And speakest only when thy soul is stirred!

THE TWO RIVERS

I

Slowly the hour-hand of the clock moves round;
So slowly that no human eye hath power
To see it move! Slowly in shine or shower
The painted ship above it, homeward bound,
Sails, but seems motionless, as if aground;
Yet both arrive at last; and in his tower
The slumberous watchman wakes and strikes the hour,
A mellow, measured, melancholy sound.
Midnight! the outpost of advancing day!
The frontier town and citadel of night!
The watershed of Time, from which the streams
Of Yesterday and To-morrow take their way,
One to the land of promise and of light,
One to the land of darkness and of dreams!

II

O River of Yesterday, with current swift
Through chasms descending, and soon lost to sight,
I do not care to follow in their flight
The faded leaves, that on thy bosom drift!
O River of To-morrow, I uplift
Mine eyes, and thee I follow, as the night
Wanes into morning, and the dawning light

Broadens, and all the shadows fade and shift!
I follow, follow, where thy waters run
Through unfrequented, unfamiliar fields,
Fragrant with flowers and musical with song;
Still follow, follow; sure to meet the sun,
And confident, that what the future yields
Will be the right, unless myself be wrong.

III

Yet not in vain, O River of Yesterday,
Through chasms of darkness to the deep descending,
I heard thee sobbing in the rain, and blending
Thy voice with other voices far away.
I called to thee, and yet thou wouldst not stay,
But turbulent, and with thyself contending,
And torrent-like thy force on pebbles spending,
Thou wouldst not listen to a poet's lay.
Thoughts, like a loud and sudden rush of wings,
Regrets and recollections of things past,
With hints and prophecies of things to be,
And inspirations, which, could they be things,
And stay with us, and we could hold them fast,
Were our good angels,—these I owe to thee.

IV

And thou, O River of To-morrow, flowing
Between thy narrow adamantine walls,
But beautiful, and white with waterfalls,
And wreaths of mist, like hands the pathway showing;
I hear the trumpets of the morning blowing,
I hear thy mighty voice, that calls and calls,
And see, as Ossian saw in Morven's halls,
Mysterious phantoms, coming, beckoning, going!
It is the mystery of the unknown
That fascinates us; we are children still,
Wayward and wistful; with one hand we cling
To the familiar things we call our own,
And with the other, resolute of will,
Grope in the dark for what the day will bring.

BOSTON

St. Bototlph's Town! Hither across the plains
And fens of Lincolnshire, in garb austere,
There came a Saxon monk, and founded here
A Priory, pillaged by marauding Danes,
So that thereof no vestige now remains;
Only a name, that, spoken loud and clear,
And echoed in another hemisphere,
Survives the sculptured walls and painted panes.
St. Botolph's Town! Far over leagues of land
And leagues of sea looks forth its noble tower,
And far around the chiming bells are heard;
So may that sacred name forever stand
A landmark, and a symbol of the power,
That lies concentred in a single word.

ST. JOHN'S, CAMBRIDGE

I stand beneath the tree, whose branches shade
Thy western window, Chapel of St. John!
And hear its leaves repeat their benison
On him, whose hand if thy stones memorial laid;
Then I remember one of whom was said
In the world's darkest hour, "Behold thy son!"
And see him living still, and wandering on
And waiting for the advent long delayed.
Not only tongues of the apostles teach
Lessons of love and light, but these expanding
And sheltering boughs with all their leaves implore,
And say in language clear as human speech,
"The peace of God, that passeth understanding,
Be and abide with you forevermore!"

MOODS

Oh that a Song would sing itself to me
Out of the heart of Nature, or the heart
Of man, the child of Nature, not of Art,
Fresh as the morning, salt as the salt sea,
With just enough of bitterness to be
A medicine to this sluggish mood, and start
The life-blood in my veins, and so impart
Healing and help in this dull lethargy!
Alas! not always doth the breath of song
Breathe on us. It is like the wind that bloweth

At its own will, not ours, nor tarries long;
We hear the sound thereof, but no man knoweth
From whence it comes, so sudden and swift and strong,
Nor whither in its wayward course it goeth.

WOODSTOCK PARK

Here in a little rustic hermitage
Alfred the Saxon King, Alfred the Great,
Postponed the cares of king-craft to translate
The Consolations of the Roman sage.
Here Geoffrey Chaucer in his ripe old age
Wrote the unrivalled Tales, which soon or late
The venturous hand that strives to imitate
Vanquished must fall on the unfinished page.
Two kings were they, who ruled by right divine,
And both supreme; one in the realm of Truth,
One in the realm of Fiction and of Song.
What prince hereditary of their line,
Uprising in the strength and flush of youth,
Their glory shall inherit and prolong?

THE FOUR PRINCESSES AT WILNA

A PHOTOGRAPH

Sweet faces, that from pictured casements lean
As from a castle window, looking down
On some gay pageant passing through a town,
Yourselves the fairest figures in the scene;
With what a gentle grace, with what serene
Unconsciousness ye wear the triple crown
Of youth and beauty and the fair renown
Of a great name, that ne'er hath tarnished been!
From your soft eyes, so innocent and sweet,
Four spirits, sweet and innocent as they,
Gaze on the world below, the sky above;
Hark! there is some one singing in the street;
"Faith, Hope, and Love! these three," he seems to say;
"These three; and greatest of the three is Love."

HOLIDAYS

The holiest of all holidays are those
Kept by ourselves in silence and apart;
The secret anniversaries of the heart,
When the full river of feeling overflows;—
The happy days unclouded to their close;
The sudden joys that out of darkness start
As flames from ashes; swift desires that dart
Like swallows singing down each wind that blows!
White as the gleam of a receding sail,
White as a cloud that floats and fades in air,
White as the whitest lily on a stream,
These tender memories are;—a Fairy Tale
Of some enchanted land we know not where,
But lovely as a landscape in a dream.

WAPENTAKE

TO ALFRED TENNYSON

Poet! I come to touch thy lance with mine;
Not as a knight, who on the listed field
Of tourney touched his adversary's shield
In token of defiance, but in sign
Of homage to the mastery, which is thine,
In English song; nor will I keep concealed,
And voiceless as a rivulet frost-congealed,
My admiration for thy verse divine.
Not of the howling dervishes of song,
Who craze the brain with their delirious dance,
Art thou, O sweet historian of the heart!
Therefore to thee the laurel-leaves belong,
To thee our love and our allegiance,
For thy allegiance to the poet's art.

THE BROKEN OAR

Once upon Iceland's solitary strand
A poet wandered with his book and pen,
Seeking some final word, some sweet Amen,
Wherewith to close the volume in his hand.
The billows rolled and plunged upon the sand,
The circling sea-gulls swept beyond his ken,
And from the parting cloud-rack now and then

Flashed the red sunset over sea and land.
Then by the billows at his feet was tossed
A broken oar; and carved thereon he read,
"Oft was I weary, when I toiled at thee";
And like a man, who findeth what was lost,
He wrote the words, then lifted up his head,
And flung his useless pen into the sea.

THE CROSS OF SNOW

In the long, sleepless watches of the night,
A gentle face—the face of one long dead—
Looks at me from the wall, where round its head
The night-lamp casts a halo of pale light.
Here in this room she died; and soul more white
Never through martyrdom of fire was led
To its repose; nor can in books be read
The legend of a life more benedight.
There is a mountain in the distant West
That, sun-defying, in its deep ravines
Displays a cross of snow upon its side.
Such is the cross I wear upon my breast
These eighteen years, through all the changing scenes
And seasons, changeless since the day she died.

ULTIMA THULE

DEDICATION TO G.W.G.

With favoring winds, o'er sunlit seas,
We sailed for the Hesperides,
The land where golden apples grow;
But that, ah! that was long ago.

How far, since then, the ocean streams
Have swept us from that land of dreams,
That land of fiction and of truth,
The lost Atlantis of our youth!

Whither, oh, whither? Are not these
The tempest-haunted Hebrides,
Where sea gulls scream, and breakers roar,
And wreck and sea-weed line the shore?

Ultima Thule! Utmost Isle!
Here in thy harbors for a while
We lower our sails; a while we rest
From the unending, endless quest.

POEMS

BAYARD TAYLOR

Dead he lay among his books!
The peace of God was in his looks.

As the statues in the gloom
Watch o'er Maximilian's tomb,

So those volumes from their shelves
Watched him, silent as themselves.

Ah! his hand will nevermore
Turn their storied pages o'er;

Nevermore his lips repeat
Songs of theirs, however sweet.

Let the lifeless body rest!
He is gone, who was its guest;

Gone, as travellers haste to leave
An inn, nor tarry until eve.

Traveller! in what realms afar,
In what planet, in what star,

In what vast, aerial space,
Shines the light upon thy face?

In what gardens of delight
Rest thy weary feet to-night?

Poet! thou, whose latest verse
Was a garland on thy hearse;

Thou hast sung, with organ tone,
In Deukalion's life, thine own;

On the ruins of the Past

Blooms the perfect flower at last.

Friend! but yesterday the bells
Rang for thee their loud farewells;

And to-day they toll for thee,
Lying dead beyond the sea;

Lying dead among thy books,
The peace of God in all thy looks!

THE CHAMBER OVER THE GATE

Is it so far from thee
Thou canst no longer see,
In the Chamber over the Gate,
That old man desolate,
Weeping and wailing sore
For his son, who is no more?
O Absalom, my son!

Is it so long ago
That cry of human woe
From the walled city came,
Calling on his dear name,
That it has died away
In the distance of to-day?
O Absalom, my son!

There is no far or near,
There is neither there nor here,
There is neither soon nor late,
In that Chamber over the Gate,
Nor any long ago
To that cry of human woe,
O Absalom, my son!

From the ages that are past
The voice sounds like a blast,
Over seas that wreck and drown,
Over tumult of traffic and town;
And from ages yet to be
Come the echoes back to me,
O Absalom, my son!

Somewhere at every hour

The watchman on the tower
Looks forth, and sees the fleet
Approach of the hurrying feet
Of messengers, that bear
The tidings of despair.
O Absalom, my son!

He goes forth from the door
Who shall return no more.
With him our joy departs;
The light goes out in our hearts;
In the Chamber over the Gate
We sit disconsolate.
O Absalom, my son!

That 't is a common grief
Bringeth but slight relief;
Ours is the bitterest loss,
Ours is the heaviest cross;
And forever the cry will be
"Would God I had died for thee,
O Absalom, my son!"

FROM MY ARM-CHAIR

TO THE CHILDREN OF CAMBRIDGE

Who presented to me on my Seventy-second Birth-day, February 27, 1879, this Chair, made from the Wood of the Village Blacksmith's Chestnut Tree.

Am I a king, that I should call my own
This splendid ebon throne?
Or by what reason, or what right divine,
Can I proclaim it mine?

Only, perhaps, by right divine of song
It may to me belong;
Only because the spreading chestnut tree
Of old was sung by me.

Well I remember it in all its prime,
When in the summer-time
The affluent foliage of its branches made
A cavern of cool shade.

There, by the blacksmith's forge, beside the street,

Its blossoms white and sweet
Enticed the bees, until it seemed alive,
And murmured like a hive.

And when the winds of autumn, with a shout,
Tossed its great arms about,
The shining chestnuts, bursting from the sheath,
Dropped to the ground beneath.

And now some fragments of its branches bare,
Shaped as a stately chair,
Have by my hearthstone found a home at last,
And whisper of the past.

The Danish king could not in all his pride
Repel the ocean tide,
But, seated in this chair, I can in rhyme
Roll back the tide of Time.

I see again, as one in vision sees,
The blossoms and the bees,
And hear the children's voices shout and call,
And the brown chestnuts fall.

I see the smithy with its fires aglow,
I hear the bellows blow,
And the shrill hammers on the anvil beat
The iron white with heat!

And thus, dear children, have ye made for me
This day a jubilee,
And to my more than three-score years and ten
Brought back my youth again.

The heart hath its own memory, like the mind,
And in it are enshrined
The precious keepsakes, into which is wrought
The giver's loving thought.

Only your love and your remembrance could
Give life to this dead wood,
And make these branches, leafless now so long,
Blossom again in song.

JUGURTHA

How cold are thy baths, Apollo!
Cried the African monarch, the splendid,
As down to his death in the hollow
Dark dungeons of Rome he descended,
Uncrowned, unthroned, unattended;
How cold are thy baths, Apollo!

How cold are thy baths, Apollo!
Cried the Poet, unknown, unbefriended,
As the vision, that lured him to follow,
With the mist and the darkness blended,
And the dream of his life was ended;
How cold are thy baths, Apollo!

THE IRON PEN

Made from a fetter of Bonnivard, the Prisoner of Chillon; the handle of wood from the Frigate
Constitution, and bound with a circlet of gold, inset with three precious stones from Siberia, Ceylon, and
Maine.

I thought this Pen would arise
From the casket where it lies—
Of itself would arise and write
My thanks and my surprise.

When you gave it me under the pines,
I dreamed these gems from the mines
Of Siberia, Ceylon, and Maine
Would glimmer as thoughts in the lines;

That this iron link from the chain
Of Bonnivard might retain
Some verse of the Poet who sang
Of the prisoner and his pain;

That this wood from the frigate's mast
Might write me a rhyme at last,
As it used to write on the sky
The song of the sea and the blast.

But motionless as I wait,
Like a Bishop lying in state
Lies the Pen, with its mitre of gold,
And its jewels inviolate.

Then must I speak, and say

That the light of that summer day
In the garden under the pines
Shall not fade and pass away.

I shall see you standing there,
Caressed by the fragrant air,
With the shadow on your face,
And the sunshine on your hair.

I shall hear the sweet low tone
Of a voice before unknown,
Saying, "This is from me to you—
From me, and to you alone."

And in words not idle and vain
I shall answer and thank you again
For the gift, and the grace of the gift,
O beautiful Helen of Maine!

And forever this gift will be
As a blessing from you to me,
As a drop of the dew of your youth
On the leaves of an aged tree.

ROBERT BURNS

I see amid the fields of Ayr
A ploughman, who, in foul and fair,
Sings at his task
So clear, we know not if it is
The laverock's song we hear, or his,
Nor care to ask.

For him the ploughing of those fields
A more ethereal harvest yields
Than sheaves of grain;
Songs flush with Purple bloom the rye,
The plover's call, the curlew's cry,
Sing in his brain.

Touched by his hand, the wayside weed
Becomes a flower; the lowliest reed
Beside the stream
Is clothed with beauty; gorse and grass
And heather, where his footsteps pass,
The brighter seem.

He sings of love, whose flame illumes
The darkness of lone cottage rooms;
He feels the force,
The treacherous undertow and stress
Of wayward passions, and no less
The keen remorse.

At moments, wrestling with his fate,
His voice is harsh, but not with hate;
The brushwood, hung
Above the tavern door, lets fall
Its bitter leaf, its drop of gall
Upon his tongue.

But still the music of his song
Rises o'er all elate and strong;
Its master-chords
Are Manhood, Freedom, Brotherhood,
Its discords but an interlude
Between the words.

And then to die so young and leave
Unfinished what he might achieve!
Yet better sure
Is this, than wandering up and down
An old man in a country town,
Infirm and poor.

For now he haunts his native land
As an immortal youth; his hand
Guides every plough;
He sits beside each ingle-nook,
His voice is in each rushing brook,
Each rustling bough.

His presence haunts this room to-night,
A form of mingled mist and light
From that far coast.
Welcome beneath this roof of mine!
Welcome! this vacant chair is thine,
Dear guest and ghost!

HELEN OF TYRE

What phantom is this that appears

Through the purple mist of the years,
Itself but a mist like these?
A woman of cloud and of fire;
It is she; it is Helen of Tyre,
The town in the midst of the seas.

O Tyre! in thy crowded streets
The phantom appears and retreats,
And the Israelites that sell
Thy lilies and lions of brass,
Look up as they see her pass,
And murmur "Jezebel!"

Then another phantom is seen
At her side, in a gray gabardine,
With beard that floats to his waist;
It is Simon Magus, the Seer;
He speaks, and she pauses to hear
The words he utters in haste.

He says: "From this evil fame,
From this life of sorrow and shame,
I will lift thee and make thee mine;
Thou hast been Queen Candace,
And Helen of Troy, and shalt be
The Intelligence Divine!"

Oh, sweet as the breath of morn,
To the fallen and forlorn
Are whispered words of praise;
For the famished heart believes
The falsehood that tempts and deceives,
And the promise that betrays.

So she follows from land to land
The wizard's beckoning hand,
As a leaf is blown by the gust,
Till she vanishes into night.
O reader, stoop down and write
With thy finger in the dust.

O town in the midst of the seas,
With thy rafts of cedar trees,
Thy merchandise and thy ships,
Thou, too, art become as naught,
A phantom, a shadow, a thought,
A name upon men's lips.

ELEGIAC

Dark is the morning with mist; in the narrow mouth of the harbor
Motionless lies the sea, under its curtain of cloud;
Dreamily glimmer the sails of ships on the distant horizon,
Like to the towers of a town, built on the verge of the sea.

Slowly and stately and still, they sail forth into the ocean;
With them sail my thoughts over the limitless deep,
Farther and farther away, borne on by unsatisfied longings,
Unto Hesperian isles, unto Ausonian shores.

Now they have vanished away, have disappeared in the ocean;
Sunk are the towers of the town into the depths of the sea!
All have vanished but those that, moored in the neighboring roadstead,
Sailless at anchor ride, looming so large in the mist.

Vanished, too, are the thoughts, the dim, unsatisfied longings;
Sunk are the turrets of cloud into the ocean of dreams;
While in a haven of rest my heart is riding at anchor,
Held by the chains of love, held by the anchors of trust!

OLD ST. DAVID'S AT RADNOR

What an image of peace and rest
Is this little church among its graves!
All is so quiet; the troubled breast,
The wounded spirit, the heart oppressed,
Here may find the repose it craves.

See, how the ivy climbs and expands
Over this humble hermitage,
And seems to caress with its little hands
The rough, gray stones, as a child that stands
Caressing the wrinkled cheeks of age!

You cross the threshold; and dim and small
Is the space that serves for the Shepherd's Fold;
The narrow aisle, the bare, white wall,
The pews, and the pulpit quaint and tall,
Whisper and say: "Alas! we are old."

Herbert's chapel at Bemerton
Hardly more spacious is than this;

But Poet and Pastor, blent in one,
Clothed with a splendor, as of the sun,
That lowly and holy edifice.

It is not the wall of stone without
That makes the building small or great
But the soul's light shining round about,
And the faith that overcometh doubt,
And the love that stronger is than hate.

Were I a pilgrim in search of peace,
Were I a pastor of Holy Church,
More than a Bishop's diocese
Should I prize this place of rest, and release
From farther longing and farther search.

Here would I stay, and let the world
With its distant thunder roar and roll;
Storms do not rend the sail that is furled;
Nor like a dead leaf, tossed and whirled
In an eddy of wind, is the anchored soul.

FOLK SONGS

THE SIFTING OF PETER

In St. Luke's Gospel we are told
How Peter in the days of old
Was sifted;
And now, though ages intervene,
Sin is the same, while time and scene
Are shifted.

Satan desires us, great and small,
As wheat to sift us, and we all
Are tempted;
Not one, however rich or great,
Is by his station or estate
Exempted.

No house so safely guarded is
But he, by some device of his,
Can enter;
No heart hath armor so complete
But he can pierce with arrows fleet
Its centre.

For all at last the cock will crow,
Who hear the warning voice, but go
Unheeding,
Till thrice and more they have denied
The Man of Sorrows, crucified
And bleeding.

One look of that pale suffering face
Will make us feel the deep disgrace
Of weakness;
We shall be sifted till the strength
Of self-conceit be changed at length
To meekness.

Wounds of the soul, though healed will ache;
The reddening scars remain, and make
Confession;
Lost innocence returns no more;
We are not what we were before
Transgression.

But noble souls, through dust and heat,
Rise from disaster and defeat
The stronger,
And conscious still of the divine
Within them, lie on earth supine
No longer.

MAIDEN AND WEATHERCOCK

MAIDEN
O weathercock on the village spire,
With your golden feathers all on fire,
Tell me, what can you see from your perch
Above there over the tower of the church?

WEATHERCOCK
I can see the roofs and the streets below,
And the people moving to and fro,
And beyond, without either roof or street,
The great salt sea, and the fisherman's fleet.

I can see a ship come sailing in
Beyond the headlands and harbor of Lynn,
And a young man standing on the deck,

With a silken kerchief round his neck.

Now he is pressing it to his lips,
And now he is kissing his finger-tips,
And now he is lifting and waving his hand
And blowing the kisses toward the land.

MAIDEN
Ah, that is the ship from over the sea,
That is bringing my lover back to me,
Bringing my lover so fond and true,
Who does not change with the wind like you.

WEATHERCOCK
If I change with all the winds that blow,
It is only because they made me so,
And people would think it wondrous strange,
If I, a Weathercock, should not change.

O pretty Maiden, so fine and fair,
With your dreamy eyes and your golden hair,
When you and your lover meet to-day
You will thank me for looking some other way.

THE WINDMILL

Behold! a giant am I!
Aloft here in my tower,
With my granite jaws I devour
The maize, and the wheat, and the rye,
And grind them into flour.

I look down over the farms;
In the fields of grain I see
The harvest that is to be,
And I fling to the air my arms,
For I know it is all for me.

I hear the sound of flails
Far off, from the threshing-floors
In barns, with their open doors,
And the wind, the wind in my sails,
Louder and louder roars.

I stand here in my place,
With my foot on the rock below,

And whichever way it may blow
I meet it face to face,
As a brave man meets his foe.

And while we wrestle and strive
My master, the miller, stands
And feeds me with his hands;
For he knows who makes him thrive,
Who makes him lord of lands.

On Sundays I take my rest;
Church-going bells begin
Their low, melodious din;
I cross my arms on my breast,
And all is peace within.

THE TIDE RISES, THE TIDE FALLS

The tide rises, the tide falls,
The twilight darkens, the curlew calls;
Along the sea-sands damp and brown
The traveller hastens toward the town,
And the tide rises, the tide falls.

Darkness settles on roofs and walls,
But the sea in the darkness calls and calls;
The little waves, with their soft, white hands,
Efface the footprints in the sands,
And the tide rises, the tide falls.

The morning breaks; the steeds in their stalls
Stamp and neigh, as the hostler calls;
The day returns, but nevermore
Returns the traveller to the shore,
And the tide rises, the tide falls.

SONNETS

MY CATHEDRAL

Like two cathedral towers these stately pines
Uplift their fretted summits tipped with cones;
The arch beneath them is not built with stones,
Not Art but Nature traced these lovely lines,

And carved this graceful arabesque of vines;
No organ but the wind here sighs and moans,
No sepulchre conceals a martyr's bones.
No marble bishop on his tomb reclines.
Enter! the pavement, carpeted with leaves,
Gives back a softened echo to thy tread!
Listen! the choir is singing; all the birds,
In leafy galleries beneath the eaves,
Are singing! listen, ere the sound be fled,
And learn there may be worship with out words.

THE BURIAL OF THE POET

RICHARD HENRY DANA

In the old churchyard of his native town,
And in the ancestral tomb beside the wall,
We laid him in the sleep that comes to all,
And left him to his rest and his renown.
The snow was falling, as if Heaven dropped down
White flowers of Paradise to strew his pall;—
The dead around him seemed to wake, and call
His name, as worthy of so white a crown.
And now the moon is shining on the scene,
And the broad sheet of snow is written o'er
With shadows cruciform of leafless trees,
As once the winding-sheet of Saladin
With chapters of the Koran; but, ah! more
Mysterious and triumphant signs are these.

NIGHT

Into the darkness and the hush of night
Slowly the landscape sinks, and fades away,
And with it fade the phantoms of the day,
The ghosts of men and things, that haunt the light,
The crowd, the clamor, the pursuit, the flight,
The unprofitable splendor and display,
The agitations, and the cares that prey
Upon our hearts, all vanish out of sight.
The better life begins; the world no more
Molests us; all its records we erase
From the dull common-place book of our lives,
That like a palimpsest is written o'er

With trivial incidents of time and place,
And lo! the ideal, hidden beneath, revives.

THE POET AND HIS SONGS

As the birds come in the Spring,
We know not from where;
As the stars come at evening
From depths of the air;

As the rain comes from the cloud,
And the brook from the ground;
As suddenly, low or loud,
Out of silence a sound;

As the grape comes to the vine,
The fruit to the tree;
As the wind comes to the pine,
And the tide to the sea;

As come the white sails of ships
O'er the ocean's verge;
As comes the smile to the lips,
The foam to the surge;

So come to the Poet his songs,
All hitherward blown
From the misty realm, that belongs
To the vast unknown.

His, and not his, are the lays
He sings; and their fame
Is his, and not his; and the praise
And the pride of a name.

For voices pursue him by day,
And haunt him by night,
And he listens, and needs must obey,
When the Angel says: "Write!"

Henry Wadsworth Longfellow – A Short Biography

Henry Wadsworth Longfellow was born on February 27th, 1807 in Portland, Maine (then part of Massachusetts) to Stephen Longfellow and Zilpah (nee Wadsworth) Longfellow. His father was a lawyer, and his maternal grandfather, Peleg Wadsworth, was a general in the American Revolutionary War and a Member of Congress.

It was a large family. Longfellow was the second of eight children; his siblings were Stephen (1805), Elizabeth (1808), Anne (1810), Alexander (1814), Mary (1816), Ellen (1818) and Samuel (1819).

Longfellow attended a dame school at the age of three and by age six was enrolled at the private Portland Academy. He was very studious and quickly became fluent in Latin. His mother encouraged his love of reading and learning and introduced him to many literary classics.

He published his first poem, a patriotic four-stanza affair entitled "The Battle of Lovell's Pond", in the Portland Gazette on November 17, 1820. He remained at the Portland Academy until he was fourteen. As a child, he spent much of his summers at his grandfather Peleg's farm in the nearby town of Hiram.

In the fall of 1822, the 15-year-old Longfellow enrolled at Bowdoin College in Brunswick, Maine. His grandfather was a founder of the college and his father a trustee. Here he met and befriended Nathaniel Hawthorne. Longfellow was already thinking of a career in literature. In his senior year he wrote to his father: "I will not disguise it in the least... the fact is, I most eagerly aspire after future eminence in literature, my whole soul burns most ardently after it, and every earthly thought centers in it... I am almost confident in believing, that if I can ever rise in the world it must be by the exercise of my talents in the wide field of literature."

Poetry was the writing form he felt most at ease with and he offered poems to many newspapers and magazines. Between January 1824 and graduation in 1825, he had almost 40 poems published, over half of which were in the short-lived Boston periodical The United States Literary Gazette.

When Longfellow graduated, he was ranked a pleasing fourth in the class, and had been elected to Phi Beta Kappa. He was quickly offered the post of professor of modern languages at his alma mater.

Accounts suggest that part of the requirement of acceptance was to tour Europe to become more immersed in both languages and cultures. Longfellow began his tour of Europe in May 1826 aboard the ship Cadmus. His travels in Europe would last three years and cost his father the princely sum of $2,604.24. He visited France, Spain, Italy, Germany and England before returning to the United States in mid-August 1829.

His stock of languages now included French, Spanish, Portuguese, and German, and impressively, mostly without any formal instruction.

On August 27th, 1829, he wrote to the president of Bowdoin that he was turning down the professorship because he considered the $600 salary "disproportionate to the duties required". The trustees countered by raising the salary to $800 and an additional $100 to serve as the college's librarian, a post which required only one hour's attention a day.

On September 14th, 1831, Longfellow married Mary Storer Potter, a childhood friend from Portland. The couple settled in Brunswick. Longfellow now published several non-fiction and fiction prose pieces inspired by his friend Washington Irving, whom he had met in Madrid during his travels, these included "The Indian Summer" and "The Bald Eagle" in 1833.

During his years teaching at the college, he translated textbooks in French, Italian and Spanish; his first published book was in 1833, a translation of the poetry of the medieval Spanish poet Jorge Manrique. A travel book, Outre-Mer: A Pilgrimage Beyond the Sea, was first published in serial form before a book edition in 1835.

In December 1834, Longfellow received a letter from Josiah Quincy III, president of Harvard College, offering him the Smith Professorship of Modern Languages with the condition that he first spend a year or so abroad. The Longfellow's set off for Europe. He would now be able to add German, Dutch, Danish, Swedish, Finnish, and Icelandic to his repertoire of languages.

During the trip they discovered that Mary was pregnant. Sadly, in October 1835, she miscarried some six months into the pregnancy. Then followed several weeks of illness and at the age of 22 on November 29th, 1835 she died. Longfellow had her body embalmed, placed in a lead coffin itself inside an oak coffin which was then shipped to Mount Auburn Cemetery near Boston. He wrote movingly "One thought occupies me night and day... She is dead—She is dead! All day I am weary and sad".

Back in the United States, Longfellow took up the professorship at Harvard. He was required to live in Cambridge, close to the campus and rented rooms at the Craigie House in the spring of 1837. The home, built in 1759, had once been the headquarters of George Washington during the Siege of Boston.

Longfellow now felt able to publish again, starting with the collection Voices of the Night in 1839. It was mainly comprised of translations together with nine original poems and seven poems written back in his teenage years.

His romantic interests also began to surface again. He had begun to court Frances 'Fanny' Appleton, daughter of the Boston industrialist Nathan Appleton. At first, the independent-minded Appleton was not interested in marriage but Longfellow was determined. In July 1839, he wrote to a friend: "Victory hangs doubtful. The lady says she will not! I say she shall! It is not pride, but the madness of passion".

In late 1839, Longfellow published Hyperion, a book in prose inspired by his trips abroad and his still un-successful courtship of Fanny Appleton. Amidst this, Longfellow fell into "periods of neurotic depression with moments of panic" and required a six-month leave of absence from Harvard to attend a health spa in the former Marienberg Benedictine Convent at Boppard in Germany.

Ballads and Other Poems was published in 1841 and included "The Village Blacksmith" and "The Wreck of the Hesperus". His reputation as a poet, and a commercial one at that, was set.

Longfellow published a play in 1842, The Spanish Student, based on his memories from his time in Spain in the 1820s. A small collection, Poems on Slavery, was also published in 1842. This was Longfellow's first public support of abolitionism. However, as Longfellow himself said, the poems were "so mild that even a Slaveholder might read them without losing his appetite for breakfast". The New England Anti-Slavery Association, however, was satisfied enough with the intent of the collection to reprint it for their own distribution.

On May 10th, 1843, after seven years in pursuit, Longfellow received a letter from Fanny Appleton agreeing to marry him. He was elated and immediately walked 90 minutes to meet her at her house.

Nathan Appleton bought the Craigie House as a wedding present to the pair. Longfellow lived there for the rest of his life. His love for Fanny is evident from Longfellow's only love poem, the sonnet "The Evening Star", written in October 1845:

"O my beloved, my sweet Hesperus!
My morning and my evening star of love!"

He once attended a ball without her and said, "The lights seemed dimmer, the music sadder, the flowers fewer, and the women less fair."

Longfellow and Fanny had six children: Charles Appleton (1844), Ernest Wadsworth (1845), Fanny (1847, who died in infancy), Alice Mary (1850), Edith (1853), and Anne Allegra (1855).

Aware of his growing stature and his ability to influence others he also encouraged and supported many other translators. In 1845, he published The Poets and Poetry of Europe, a large 800-page compendium of translated works by other writers. Longfellow intended the anthology "to bring together, into a compact and convenient form, as large an amount as possible of those English translations which are scattered through many volumes, and are not accessible to the general reader".

On November 1st, 1847, the epic poem Evangeline was published.

Longfellow's literary income was now becoming quite substantial: in 1840, he had made $219 but by 1850 it had grown to a very promising $1,900.

On June 14th, 1853, Longfellow held a farewell dinner party at his Cambridge home for his great friend Nathaniel Hawthorne, who was preparing to move overseas.

In 1854, Longfellow retired from Harvard, devoting himself entirely to writing. He would be awarded an honorary doctorate of laws from Harvard in 1859.

The Song of Haiwatha, his epic poem, and perhaps his best known and enjoyed work was published in 1855.

On a hot July 9th day, 1861, Fanny was putting several locks of her children's hair into an envelope and making attempts to seal it with hot sealing wax while Longfellow took a nap. The circumstances of what happened next vary but the actuality is that Fanny's dress caught fire. Her screams awakened Longfellow who rushed to help her and threw a rug over her and stifled the flames with his own body as best he could, but Fanny was already horrifically burned.

A doctor was called and Fanny was taken to her room to recover. She was in and out of consciousness throughout the night and was also administered ether. The next morning, July 10th, 1861, she died shortly after 10 o'clock after asking for a cup of coffee.

Longfellow, in his effort to save her had also been badly burned and was unable to attend her funeral. His facial injuries required he stopped shaving. The ensuing beard now became the quintessential look that everyone remembers from pictures.

Devastated, he never fully recovered and sometimes resorted to laudanum and ether to ease the pain. He worried he would go insane and begged "not to be sent to an asylum" and noted that he was "inwardly bleeding to death". In the sonnet "The Cross of Snow" (1879), which he wrote eighteen years later he wrote:

"Such is the cross I wear upon my breast
These eighteen years, through all the changing scenes
And seasons, changeless since the day she died".

Longfellow spent several years translating Dante Alighieri's epic poem, The Divine Comedy. To aid him in perfecting the translation and reviewing proofs, he invited several friends to weekly meetings every Wednesday from 1864. This became known as the "Dante Club", and regulars included William Dean Howells, James Russell Lowell, Charles Eliot Norton and other occasional guests. The full three-volume translation was published in the spring of 1867, though Longfellow would continue to revise it. It was wildly popular and was re-printed four times in its first year.

By 1868, Longfellow's annual income was over a staggering $48,000.

Longfellow was also part of a group of Poets who became known as The Fireside Poets. The group included Longfellow, William Cullen Bryant, John Greenleaf Whittier, James Russell Lowell, and Oliver Wendell Holmes Snr. Occasionally Ralph Waldo Emerson is also placed among their number. The name "Fireside Poets" derives from poetry reading as a collective family entertainment of the times.

During the 1860s, Longfellow, still a committed abolitionist, also hoped for a coming together, a reconciliation, between the north and south after the dark days of the Civil War. When his son was wounded during the war, he wrote the poem "Christmas Bells", later the basis of the carol I Heard the Bells on Christmas Day.

In 1874, Samuel Cutler Ward helped him sell the poem "The Hanging of the Crane" to the New York Ledger for $3,000; it was the highest price ever paid for a poem. An astonishing sum. But Longfellow was worth it. His fame and audience were widespread and devoted.

Continuing in his hopes for a better and more united America he wrote in his journal in 1878: "I have only one desire; and that is for harmony, and a frank and honest understanding between North and South". Longfellow, despite his aversion to public speaking, took up an offer from Joshua Chamberlain to speak at his fiftieth reunion at Bowdoin College. Here he read the poem "Morituri Salutamus" so quietly that few could hear.

On August 22th, 1879, a female admirer who seemed to know little about his history, traveled to Longfellow's house in Cambridge and, unaware to whom she was speaking, asked Longfellow: "Is this the house where Longfellow was born?" Longfellow told her it was not. The visitor then asked if he had died here. "Not yet", he replied.

Much of Longfellow's work is recognized for its melody-like musicality. As he says, "what a writer asks of his reader is not so much to like as to listen".

Longfellow, like many others of the period, called for the development of high quality American literature. In his work, Kavanagh, a character says: "We want a national literature commensurate with our mountains and rivers... We want a national epic that shall correspond to the size of the country... We want a national drama in which scope shall be given to our gigantic ideas and to the unparalleled activity of our people... In a word, we want a national literature altogether shaggy and unshorn, that shall shake the earth, like a herd of buffaloes thundering over the prairies."

As a translator Longfellow was very impressive. His translation of Dante's The Divine Comedy became a requirement for those who wanted to be a part of high culture.

In 1874, Longfellow oversaw a 31-volume anthology called Poems of Places, collecting poems of several geographical locations; Europe, Asia, and the Arabian countries. It was a work of great educational endeavor but Emerson was disappointed and is said to have told Longfellow: "The world is expecting better things of you than this... You are wasting time that should be bestowed upon original production".

At this point in his life Longfellow could look back and see that his early collections, Voices of the Night and Ballads and Other Poems, had made him instantly popular. The New-Yorker called him "one of the very few in our time who has successfully aimed in putting poetry to its best and sweetest uses". The Southern Literary Messenger immediately put Longfellow "among the first of our American poets".

The rapidity with which American readers embraced Longfellow was unparalleled in publishing history in the United States. His popularity spread throughout Europe, his poems translated into Italian, French, German, and other languages.

Longfellow was the most popular poet of his day. As a friend once wrote to him, "no other poet was so fully recognized in his lifetime". Some of his works including "Paul Revere's Ride" and "The Song of Haiwatha" may have rewritten the facts but became essential parts of the American psyche and culture. He was so admired that on his 70th birthday in 1877 the atmosphere was that of a national holiday, with parades, speeches, and, of course, the reading of his poems.

Over the years, Longfellow's reputation came to include his personality; he was a gentle, placid, poetic soul. James Russell Lowell said, Longfellow had an "absolute sweetness, simplicity, and modesty". The reality was that Longfellow's life was much more difficult than was assumed. He suffered from neuralgia, which caused him constant pain, and poor eyesight. The difficulties of coping with the loss of two wives also took its toll. He was very quiet, reserved, and private; in later years, he became increasingly unsocial and avoided leaving home if he could.

In March 1882, Longfellow went to bed with severe stomach pain. He endured the pain for several days with the help of opium.

Henry Wadsworth Longfellow died, surrounded by family, on Friday, March 24th, 1882. He had been suffering from peritonitis.

He is buried with both of his wives at Mount Auburn Cemetery in Cambridge, Massachusetts. At Longfellow's funeral, his friend Ralph Waldo Emerson called him "a sweet and beautiful soul".

At the time of his death, his estate was valued at $356,320.

In 1884, Longfellow became the first non-British writer for whom a sculpted bust was placed in Poet's Corner of Westminster Abbey in London; he remains the sole American poet thus represented.

Henry Wadsworth Longfellow – A Concise Bibliography

Outre-Mer: A Pilgrimage Beyond the Sea (Travelogue) (1835)
Hyperion, a Romance (1839)
The Spanish Student. A Play in Three Acts (1843)
Evangeline: A Tale of Acadie (poem) (1847)
Kavanagh (1849)
The Golden Legend (poem) (1851)
The Song of Hiawatha (poem) (1855)
The New England Tragedies (1868)
The Divine Tragedy (1871)
Christus: A Mystery (1872)
Aftermath (poem) (1873)
The Arrow and the Song (poem)

Poetry Collections

Voices of the Night (1839)
Ballads & Other Poems (1841)
Poems on Slavery (1842)
The Belfry of Bruges & Other Poems (1845)
The Seaside and the Fireside (1850)
The Poetical Works of Henry Wadsworth Longfellow (1852)
The Courtship of Miles Standish & Other Poems (1858)
Tales of a Wayside Inn (1863)
Birds of Passage (1863)
Household Poems (1865)
Flower-de-Luce (1867)
Three Books of Song (1872)
The Masque of Pandora & Other Poems (1875)
Kéramos & Other Poems (1878)
Ultima Thule (1880)
In the Harbor (1882)
Michel Angelo: A Fragment (incomplete; published posthumously)

Translations

Coplas de Don Jorge Manrique (Translation from Spanish) (1833)
Dante's Divine Comedy (Translation) (1867)

Anthologies

Poets and Poetry of Europe (Translations) (1845)
The Waif (1845)
Poems of Places (1874)

www.ingramcontent.com/pod-product-compliance
Lightning Source LLC
Chambersburg PA
CBHW060056050426
42448CB00011B/2486